W9-CDI-214

"Boys and girls," Ms. Mackle said. "It's time to work together to make something and then write about it. I want you to show how people lived in the Old West."

"Why does Harry have to work with us?"
Sidney said. "He isn't good at making things."

"Come on," Mary said. "We're all good friends."

"I'll make the log house," Mary said.

"I'll make some things that people wore in the Old West," said Ida.

"I'll make some plants," Song Lee said.

"I'll make some animals," Sidney said.

"I'll help you," Harry said.

"Look!" said Harry to Mary and Ida.

"What's that, Harry?" they both asked.

"It's a fish," said Harry.

"A fish?" said Ida.

"What does a fish have to do with the Old West?"
Sidney asked.

"People in the Old West had to eat, didn't they?"
Harry said. "They took fish from the lakes."

"They wouldn't want to eat THAT fish!"
Sidney said.

"Sidney," Song Lee said. "We need Harry's fish.
Fish help plants to grow. If we put Harry's fish
in the ground, it will help our plants to grow."
So Harry and Song Lee put the fish in the ground.

Mary made a lake. Ida made a pretty blouse,
a black dress, and other things that people
wore in the Old West.

"Look!" said Harry.

"What's that, Harry?" they all asked.

"It's a chicken," said Harry.

"What does a chicken have to do with the Old West?" asked Sidney.

"People in the Old West had to eat, didn't they?" said Harry.

"Harry!" Sidney said. "Is that all you ever think about?"

Harry picked up another mound of clay.
"You just made me think of another thing to make!"
Harry said. "Thanks, Sidney!"

Song Lee took Harry's clay chicken and
made it look a little more like a chicken that
people would eat.

"What are you doing, Harry?" Sidney asked.

"Sitting on my clay," said Harry.

"WHAT?" said the others.

"I'm making the clay flat," said Harry.

"Now that the clay is nice and flat, I'm going to make dishes," said Harry.

"Dishes?" they all said.

"People in the Old West had to eat off something, didn't they?" said Harry.

"You're right, Harry!" said Song Lee.

"That sounds good to me," Mary said.

"This is all very good!" said Ms. Mackle.
"You even have dishes for the people! How did you ever come up with that?"

"Sidney helped me think of it," Harry said.

"I did?" Sidney said.

"I'm happy you are helping each other so much," Ms. Mackle said. "I know that you're all dear friends, and it shows. You're doing great work!"

"We are?" Sidney said.

Ms. Mackle was right. Good friends do work well together.